Inspirational Coloring Book

This Book Belongs To:

Good things
TAKE
TIME

Life
is
Beautiful

Focus
on the
good

All you need is love

Brave

TRUST

CHOOSE
JOY

You
so
are Loved

Don't
Give
UP

I can
and
I will

NEVER
Stop
Trying

THE
best
THINGS
IN
LIFE
ARE
NOT
things

Today is a
GOOD
DAY

Time to
Shine

Trust
Yourself

I Believe in You

Love is All

You are
the
Best

have a nice Day

You make me Proud

Love
is all Around

hope

Make it happen
LOVE

Never
look
back

Keep
it
COOL

Love
You make me happy

INSPIRE

no rain
no flowers

Be Kind

Laugh
Daily

Choose
LOVE

Follow
your heart

Stay
Positive

Let
love
GROW

Be the Light
You're amazing

Begin
AGAIN

HAPPY
Mind
HAPPY
Life

Never
Settle

Be Strong
BELIEVE in YOURSELF

Everything
is
GONNA
BE
Alright

TO BE HAPPY
IS A
CHOICE
WE
MAKE

All you need is LOVE

have a
nice
life

let's
get
lost

All you need is LOVE

do
what
you
love

Write it
on you heart
that
every day is
the best day
of the year
- Ralph Waldo -
Emerson

What is a weed?
A plant whose virtues have never been discovered
Ralph Waldo Emerson

DO NOt
BE ANXIOUS
about
anything
Philippians 4:5

Made in the USA
Columbia, SC
16 November 2020

24651306R00057